WINNING without WINNING:
Coaching kids to a positive attitude in sports... and in life

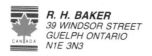

R. H. BAKER
39 WINDSOR STREET
GUELPH ONTARIO
N1E 3N3

WINNING
without
WINNING

Gerry Crowley

(with Gabriella Currie)

A Hearthstone Book
FROM THE MERCURY PRESS

The publisher gratefully acknowledges the financial assistance of the Canada Council and the Ontario Arts Council in its ongoing operations.

AUTHOR'S ACKNOWLEDGEMENT
Many thanks to Rivercrest Publishers, whose support, assistance and belief in this project made this book possible.

Cover photographs by Scott Wishart (details)
Interior illustrations by John Ashby
Cover design by Orange Griffin
Composition and page design by TASK

Printed and bound in Canada
Printed on acid-free paper

1 2 3 4 5 01 00 99 98 97

Canadian Cataloguing in Publication

Crowley, Gerry, 1953–
Winning without winning : a practical guide for coaches and parents
ISBN 1-55128-043-4
1. Sports for children - Psychological aspects. I. Title.
GV709.2.C76 1997   796'.083   C97-930477-6

Distributed in Canada by General Distribution Services
Distributed in the U.S. by LPC Group

The Mercury Press
2569 Dundas Street West
Toronto, Ontario
Canada   M6P 1X7

For Catherine, my wife
With my everlasting love, for believing
in me, and for inspiring me
to believe in myself.

ACKNOWLEDGEMENTS

Writing this book was perhaps the most difficult endeavour of my life. But the seemingly endless hours and the emotional roller-coaster created a magic for me—real magic, because of the support from so many people who, in one way or another, contributed to the book's evolution.
I name but a few:

Rick Vogel, for without him the book would still be just a thought.

Paul Low, for being my role model.

Denis Trudeau, a friend who is always there.

John Ashby, for creative illustrations which saved a million words.

Gabriella Currie, for her belief, insights, clarity, and writing skills.

Harry Currie, my catalyst and my editor.

Kyle and Joshua Smith, two little boys, brothers aged five and three, who may never realize the positive effect they have had on my life. They prove the dictum that 'by the children we shall be taught.'

My family and my friends, for the unconditional support which made *Winning without Winning* possible.

— *Gerry Crowley*

A NOTE ON THE TEXT

Throughout this book the pronoun "he" has been used to describe both coaches and the children on their teams. This was done for simplicity's sake only, to avoid unwieldy double pronouns. The findings, precepts, anecdotes and suggestions in this book are intended to apply equally to all players and coaches— girls and boys, men and women— involved in all minor sports.

Contents

INTRODUCTION

"My hat is in the ring." — *Theodore Roosevelt*

I know it, and you know it: a problem exists in minor sports. Countless interpretations abound, but when all is said and done, there is one central problem.

That problem is a focus on *winning* at all costs, and this problem does not start with the children.

As a youngster I participated in minor sports. Like all children, I experienced some good times and times I'd rather forget. I grew up, got married, and had children of my own. Then, as many people do, I continued to participate in minor sports— this time as a coach. I love sports, and I love coaching kids.

After several years of coaching, the minor sports organization to which I was attached invited me to join their executive. As a member of the governing board, I went to more and more games and tournaments at a variety of age levels, from those played by four-year-olds just learning rudimentary physical skills to those featuring the league's adolescent all-stars. I had gone from deeply involved, subjective participant— player, then coach— to deeply involved— and then deeply concerned— observer. Something was awry. Violence broke out at games; officials were verbally abused, and parents, and kids were, as well; some people even had to be ejected. Most important, many children dragged themselves dejectedly off the field after games. The atmosphere was too often tense, nervous, and unhappy. The kids simply wanted to have fun— that's why they were on the field— but the adults were keen on a different objective— winning!

In order to gather as much data as I could, I attended hundreds of games in various minor sports for both girls and boys. What was I hoping to find? I wasn't sure, but I knew there had to be a common element. I spoke with children, coaches, parents and other league organizers. I took notes and asked for input and eventually received more than 4000 letters from those involved at different levels of minor sports. The most moving were from adults who relayed to me their experiences as children. Their childhood memories of events during their days as minor sports players were sharp and clear, and in many cases had affected their adult lives.

I wanted to do something about this problem. It is my hope that by creating an awareness of what is happening, of what children are learning and the resultant detrimental effects, we can redefine the philosophy of minor sports and, once again, enjoy a healthy perspective within it.

This book is about children. Our children today depend on us— the adults— for their every need, but tomorrow they will be the adults making their own decisions. The actions they take tomorrow depend directly on the actions we take today.

Children need to play and to have fun. Studies have shown that they learn more and perform better when they enjoy what they are doing. There is so much our children can learn from minor organized sports, not the least of which should be to feel good about their own personal accomplishments and their contributions to the team as a whole. As parents and coaches and officials it is our job to set examples. We need to become aware of what winning really is, to understand how to make all children feel like winners— for the sake of the children. And are they not those for whom we toil?

Applying what I have learned to coaching children is not magic.

It's attitude. And it works!

I: THE WAKE-UP CALL

"If you can keep your head when all about you are losing
theirs . . . then you will be a man, my son."
— *Rudyard Kipling*

I had a theory, albeit an untested one, and I was excited about gathering support for it. Each year at the season-end tournament there were fights and ejections. One year, during the six-year-old age level events, a parent became so abusive he had to be removed from the field by police. Can you imagine the looks on the faces of the players when an adult was placed in a police cruiser and taken away? How must his own child have felt? I was determined that this should never happen again.

To that end I held a seminar focusing on a new perspective awareness. Twenty-eight adults attended, most of them coaches. The results might surprise some, but I found them gratifyingly predictable.

I began by welcoming everyone to a new idea— winning without winning. I explained that my goal was to make adults aware of what was required of them when they decided to coach children.

I started by asking: "What are a coach's duties?"

A discussion followed about being on time, having the equipment there, etc. Then I asked a different kind of question: "What should coaches be teaching children?" The lively dialogue that resulted suggested I had hit a nerve.

I then had each participant write down a list of five things coaches should teach kids. (We'll discuss these in detail later in this book.) Perhaps it seems silly, picturing twenty-eight adults sitting around writing their thoughts down on a piece of paper as though it were a school classroom, but this type of brainstorming is used in business and industry at the highest planning levels.

I had given an enormous amount of thought to the planning of my seminar. I realized that an idea is not really your own until you have written it down. It is certainly too easy to forget unless you see it in black and white. How often are you driving in the car or just drifting off to sleep and something really important pops into your mind? You think you'll remember it later, or in the morning, but most often it simply vanishes from your thoughts— unless you write it down.

So each individual picked up his or her pencil and began. The only stipulation was that they had to begin with the sentence "I believe coaches should be teaching kids..." and then continue with the list. While they were writing, you could hear a pin drop. During our discussion, and after, the feedback was fantastic. In fact, the next day I had one coach call to tell me that because of that seminar she and her

Having fun nurtures inner strength. A child cannot help but smile.

daughter were, once again, on good terms. It had been two weeks since they had spoken to each other.

It bears repeating that I was not surprised by the overall sense and understanding that prevailed at that seminar, but I was very pleased.

The proof of the pudding is in the eating, and at that year's final tournament a new attitude emerged. Most coaches remembered that the children were there to improve personal skills and, above all, to have fun. I had determined to be present at all games involving problem coaches. I remember clearly the incident I'm about to recall as though it were unfolding before me.

The umpire was out of position and made an indisputably incorrect call. The defensive team was up in arms and I was all set for trouble. Then the unexpected happened. The coach called his infield together at the pitcher's mound and in a loud voice proclaimed, "Boys, we're here to have fun. Forget the call." Forget the call? We were all dumbstruck. Mouths dropped and eyes blinked in disbelief. A look of wonder appeared on the faces of the kids. A bad call by an umpire didn't matter?

What a pleasant change from angry words, elevated stress levels, tears, hurt feelings and damaged egos. Simple words that demonstrated a simple philosophy, spoken by a man who, days earlier, would have lost his temper. And all because, at our seminar, he had become aware of his inappropriate behaviour.

I knew I had something here. Magic? Miracle? Whatever you call it, this simple philosophy needed to find its audience.

So, after countless meetings, endless discussions, and an unfaltering belief, this book was created.

FOR PARENTS AND COACHES

Make your own list of what you think coaches should be teaching children. As you work through this book, compare and consider what you have written with what is presented in these pages. Compare notes with colleagues and parents. Expand and amend your list to suit your own situation and to include practical examples that relate directly to your own organization.

II: YO! WHAT'S UP?

"In youth we learn; in age we understand."
— *Marie Ebner-Eschenbach*

There is a problem in minor sports. Ever increasing rumblings from coaches, spectators, game officials and participants themselves indicate the problem's magnitude. You've only to check your local newspaper for letters to the editor to confirm this. Something is wrong, and it permeates every facet of minor sports, regardless of activity, gender or age.

The header read "Baseball Season Taught Poor Lessons for Life" when the following letter to the editor appeared in a Canadian newspaper.

My fifteen-year-old son has been playing minor baseball and minor hockey since he was six, yet I have never been so discouraged as during this past poorly organized season. Nor have I seen such a display of outbursts and bad temper.

To begin, my pre-registration cheque was mailed in December and cashed in January. Then we waited.

In the past, ball practices have normally begun at the end of April or beginning of May. This year, my son waited for weeks for a call from a coach to say when practices would begin, when his first game would be played and what team he would play on.

At the end of May, after several messages I left on an answering machine, I was informed that, sorry, they didn't have coaches! Should sports organizations that have cashed one's cheque months in advance not have the courtesy to at least inform players of the situation about coaches and other arrangements? When finally we were on a team, they informed us that there would be no practices— there were no ball diamonds available.

When the season finally got under way, arguments broke out at several of the games. Several others were rained out. Those were to be rescheduled, yet at the last game of the season we were informed that the rained-out games were not going to be played.

And let me tell you about that last game. Before it began, an umpire, who was not officiating that day, got into an argument with the coaches. Then he left, and the game began. About halfway through another argument broke out, this time between the two game umpires and the coaches. There were tense moments. Words were exchanged and I wondered if they were going to come to blows! Finally, the umpire told the children to go home— the game was over.

Those children begged him. They pleaded, 'It's our last game. Please, let us play.' But the game was over.

Minor sports aren't cheap. I paid for my son to play ball for a full season. I feel he has been cheated and should be reimbursed for the failure to reschedule certain games.

What has this season taught our children? 'It's okay, we have your money. Nothing you can do about it.' It has taught the children to swear, argue, raise their tempers and come close to fist fights. Whatever happened to good sportsmanship and going out to have a good time?

Three strikes— you're out. I feel that the three strikes came before the season even started.

What did happen to good sportsmanship and going out to have a good time? I'm sure you feel this parent's frustration as personally as I do. Her complaints are valid— her son learned negative values from his experience with minor sports that season. It is beyond sad that those boys wanted so desperately just to play ball and instead, through circumstances that had nothing to do with them, their last game of the season was cancelled.

Children are full of enthusiasm and optimism. Life, to them, is full of possibilities. The memory of a caught fly-ball, played on a loop again and again in their minds, will last forever. This is the stuff dreams are made of. Yet we tamper with those dreams by abusing the positions of authority we are in. We, the parents and coaches, have the power to build or to destroy, and that is an awesome responsibility.

As with every story, there are two sides, so in the interests of fair play I have included the umpire's response to that parent's letter, which appeared in the letters to the editor section some days later.

I would like to come to an understanding with 'Pat' about her letter entitled, 'Baseball Season Taught Poor Lessons for Life.'

Considering how many leagues there are in this area, baseball diamonds are in short supply. League convenors won't know how many diamonds they are going to get until the city tells them. Coaches are volunteers who offer their time. They, too, are in limited supply.

'Pat's' money covers the cost of maintaining the diamonds, such as putting the lines down, and paying umpiring fees so she can have umpires at the games. Being an umpire in one hundred or so games this year, I am judge, jury and executioner out on the playing field. An umpire pays for his own equipment and is out there as much to serve the children playing baseball as are the coaches, but paid to know the rules. Umpires don't like ejections or forfeits either, for the same reason 'Pat' cited about what they teach children. Umpires are human. We make mistakes, but that's life. Some of the rules call for ejection and/or game forfeiture as a way of calming down a situation such as the one cited by 'Pat.' There is nothing else an umpire can do, according to the rule book.

Why doesn't 'Pat' become a coach? Failing that, she could become an umpire. She would have a greater appre-

ciation for all that goes on behind the scenes rather than complaining about it.

Coaches are volunteers— true. Umpires serve children for much the same reason as do coaches— true. Umpires make mistakes— true. Umpires are human— true. Yet, in all of this some very important details have been overlooked. What lessons are the children learning? Who controls what the children learn? When does the fun begin?

In his response the umpire states that game ejection and game forfeiture are necessary to calm certain situations down. That begs the questions of why we create situations that escalate through anger, necessitating an umpire's drastic interventions. It matters very little who is right and who is wrong. Do we want to teach our children that ranting and raving are the way to handle anger?

Children are constantly learning. The younger they are the more impressionable they are. It is our job to present children with positive learning experiences, not negative ones. The example that we set is the lead children will follow.

Consider this scenario.

A mother and her son are in an elevator. Suddenly, the lights go out and the elevator shudders to a halt. The child is about to panic and tears well up in his eyes. He calls to his mother who has remained calm and reassures him that everything is all right. Help is on the way. She gives him a hug and his world is safe once again. He trusts her and follows her lead until the situation is resolved. This lesson will be stored in the child's memory to become a part of his coping mechanism. However, had she behaved irrationally—screaming and crying in terror— you can bet that that too would have been burned into the child's memory, giving him quite a different set of coping skills for life. We often take our own actions for granted, not realizing that they have a direct impact on a child's state of mind, now and for the future.

The same lesson applies to the relationship between a coach and his team. If the coach is out to win at all costs, his team will believe that they, too, must win at all costs. If the coach gets angry and throws equipment, his team will learn that when they get angry they, too, can throw equipment. It is paramount in life for each one of us to learn to deal constructively with our anger, because anger leads to... I'll let you finish the sentence.

If the coach complains and yells at the officials, then his team will also feel they can complain and yell at the officials. A child's developing sense of logic might tell him that if it's okay to yell at an official, then it must also be okay to yell at his teacher, or his parents, or worse.

Are you getting the picture? The corollary of each of these is a negative lesson learned for life. These children then carry these lessons into other aspects of their lives and on into adulthood. It's called a transference of learning. It stands to reason that teaching positive attitudes about sports instils positive values about the game of life. Make no mistake— a coach's obsession to win at all costs will cripple the developing psyche of a child.

FOR PARENTS AND COACHES

Briefly note down experiences that you had as children involved in minor sports that affected you or others negatively. Consider how the negative events could have been handled differently by the adults to provide a positive outcome.

Then write down recent experiences in the lives of your children and the children you coach that probably had a similar impact. Consider and then note down ways in which these events could have been handled differently.

III: HEROES, HEROINES, EVERY ONE!

"If Hero mean 'sincere man,' why may not every one of us be a Hero?" — *Carlyle*

In all my research, never once did I see it written that a hero is the winner of a game. The root of the word "hero" is Greek in origin and it means, simply, protector. Or, as the dictionary tells us, a hero is someone who is admired for his brave and noble deeds. Every day there are noble deeds performed by ordinary people like you and me. We are all heroes who strive to be kind and helpful in our everyday lives. So being a hero doesn't necessarily mean hitting a home run, scoring the winning goal, or dunking a three-pointer from centre line. Doing something right for the team makes you just as much a hero. Trying, against all odds, makes you a hero.

Jesse is a pretty typical eleven-year-old boy who loves

baseball and plays little league every year. He isn't the best player on his team, but he's not the worst either. During one particular game, Jesse was standing out in right field waiting anxiously for the next pitch. Smack! A line-drive to right field. Jesse held his breath and charged the ball, hoping to make a shoestring catch to end the inning. But the ball hit

Jesse felt like a hero.

the ground just inches from his outstretched glove. Jesse stretched some more and the ball short-hopped right into his glove. The runner on first base, by this time, was rounding second base on his way to third. Instinct took over and Jesse fired the ball to third base. The bullet was knee high and in time. We all expected an out, but the third baseman dropped the ball. The runner was safe but Jesse didn't care. He had never thrown the ball so fast and so true in his life and this was his moment of glory. Umpires and spectators stood cheering and applauding. They knew they had seen something that rarely happens in minor league play.

The inning was up and the team ran back to the dug-out. Everyone was cheering Jesse's effort again and he grinned from ear to ear. He felt like Joe Carter. Jesse felt like a hero! If only the story ended there.

Unfortunately, Jesse's play was not part of the team repertoire. He was supposed to use the cut-off man.

"That's not what we practised!" the coach yelled.

And then he chewed Jesse out in the finest tradition of malevolence, spewing his venom on his unsuspecting victim whose greatest effort now was trying to hold back the tears.

What could have been— should have been— a memory of a lifetime will now be remembered as a moment of incredible humiliation for poor Jesse. Each time he casts his recollections back to that day, he'll wonder. Jesse will either rise above the moment and understand that the coach was wrong in what he did, or he'll forever look to others for the 'right' decision, not trusting his own instinct. I can't imagine being the person responsible for damaging the delicate psyche of that child.

Jesse was a hero that day because he had achieved a personal best. Everybody knew it except for one dangerous coach who had lost his perspective-awareness.

**Yup! My best catch ever! Hmm...
I wonder if we won that game?**

I have gotten letters about various experiences in minor sports from all over the world. Some expressed memories of positive import while others still felt the discomfort of a hurtful experience. Yet all the letters had one thing in common. The writer could not remember the outcome of the game! Could it be that there can be moments of triumph within a game, even if the loss of the game is inevitable? Your coaching will create memories. What kind of memories?

The outcome of the game is insignificant compared to what a child can really learn from your coaching. Your conduct will directly influence a child's attitude, and that attitude the child will carry with him for the rest of his life. This attitude will pervade every decision he makes, perhaps even as to how he will treat his own children. You have that power. It's an awesome responsibility.

FOR PARENTS AND COACHES

Consider whether your efforts are focused on *winning* every game and only winning every game, and what effect this aim is having on the children involved.

IV: TINKER, TAILOR, SOLDIER, SAILOR

"He is wise who can instruct us and assist us in the business of daily virtuous living." —Carlyle

Many adults wind up as coaches by default. This happened during my son's first year of soccer. Like a tail with no dog, fifteen eager children turned up for the first practice of the year, only to be told by members of the executive that unless a parent volunteered to coach, we all might just as well go home— there would be no team this year. Try to explain that to a seven-year-old. Yet this happens all too often.

If you've picked up this book because you've decided to volunteer as a little league coach, bravo! Without people like you there would be scores of bored, unmotivated children hanging about. Well, perhaps I exaggerate, but yours is a very generous gesture and, for all its problems, minor sports play an important role in the development of children. Remember, though, that coaching is a responsibility that goes far beyond the physical skills of a child. Are you up for it?

Let's examine the duties and responsibilities that go along with the position. Unfortunately, while most minor sports organizations have a constitution that describes in detail the duties of each member of its executive, nothing exists to help coaches. Start by asking yourself, "What should I be teaching the children?" Take a few moments to consider the answer and write your thoughts down. Seeing these ideas on paper, in your own handwriting, is so much more meaningful than just thinking about them.

It's important to remember that children all develop differently. Some will have physical talents that may very well determine their path in life. But for most children, attitude will be what determines not only where they go in life, but also how they handle life's ups and downs. To someone with a positive attitude, the sun shines each day. You're probably asking what attitude has to do with coaching.

The dictionary defines a coach as someone who trains athletes, and defines an athlete as someone who is strong, vigorous and muscular. But not all children are athletes. Children are unfinished business— works-in-progress that need nurturing and guidance. A coach must be a teacher, a leader and a role model.

There has been much said in the media today about the importance of role models. Professional athletes like Donovan Bailey, Michael Jordan, 'Magic' Johnson, Marnie McBean, Doug Gilmour, Josée Chouinard, Dave Winfield, etc., recognize the responsibility they carry because they are idolized by young boys and girls. Their actions are scrutinized because that is what children do. They mimic without knowing that's what they're doing. There is none so observant of detail as a child!

As a coach in minor sports, your influence on these impressionable innocents is even more important, because you are *real*. You are a part of their lives in a tangible way and your contact with them has direct cause and effect. Unfortunately, some coaches are more concerned with their own reputations than with the real matter of developing growth experiences through participation in sports.

There are approximately four-hundred-thousand active coaches across the country, each with about fifteen children on a team. You do the math. It means that there is an astronomical number of lessons being passed on each year, and many of these stymie self-esteem and confidence.

Unfortunately, few coaches come equipped with much more than the basic knowledge of the game they are coaching. They put too much emphasis on winning. So, what should you be teaching the children? Read on.

FOR PARENTS AND COACHES

Ask yourself whether or not coaches and parents in your sports organization allow their own needs or egos to supersede the needs of the children. Are there ways to address this and related issues within your organization?

V: I LOVE THESE LITTLE PEOPLE

"For titles do not reflect honor on men, but rather men on their titles." — Machiavelli

Is it possible to come up with a consensus of a list of lessons, or precepts, which coaches should pass on to the children? I have asked the question at each seminar I've organized and each lecture I've given. Here, then, is a list, in ranking order, of the twenty responses offered most often. It's important to remember that these are the choices of a cross-section of the people involved in minor sports— including parents, officials, league executives and coaches— and therefore a reasonable representation of opinion.

Sportsmanship
Physical Skill
Teamwork

Learning the Game
Being Fair
Having Fun
Discipline and Self-control
Motivation
How to Win
Leadership
How to Compete
Physical Fitness
Patience
Respect
Reliability
How to Lose
Responsibility
Setting Goals
Resilience
Perspective

There is an indisputable link between participation in sports and building self-esteem, provided, of course, that the experience is a positive one. Without self-esteem, it is said that a child can never properly develop strength of character. Child psychologists have determined that there are also a great many indirect benefits, such as a sense of belonging that comes from joining with team members for a common goal and a feeling of satisfaction knowing that you are important to your team and that they like you. The American sports psychologist, Dr. Eric Margenau, summed it up beautifully when he wrote: "For society in general, sports creates a reason for people to come together, for sharing a communality of experience, for developing self-esteem, and for enriching the inner life through fantasy."

Now ask yourself again, "What should I be teaching the children?" Take another look at the list of lessons put together by coaches just like you, and you must conclude, as I did, that your instinct is right.

These lessons seem a long way from the "win at all costs" philosophy that so many minor sports coaches embrace. I emphasize minor sports because it's important to distinguish the objectives of minor sports from those of major league sports, although here, too, events cause us to think twice. I would be remiss if I did not digress briefly in order to present what is considered to be an unusual attitude for professionals.

Golfer Greg Norman lost at the 1996 Masters golf tournament. Norman had a six-shot lead and blew it in the fourth round. One sports reporter called it "One of the biggest chokes."

But Norman came out a hero by gracefully accepting the defeat as one of life's unexpected trials. "It's not the end of the world," he said. "I'll get up tomorrow morning still breathing, I hope."

An editorial in the *New York Times* empathized: "Anyone who has ever flubbed a job interview, gone blank in the middle of delivering a speech, or double-faulted to lose a set, can identify with Greg Norman."

In 1987, the incomparable Boris Becker, the youngest

Wimbledon winner ever, lost to a young Australian. Reporters clambered to record Becker's public suffering.

"Is this your most disappointing defeat ever?" cried one reporter.

"No, I've lost tougher matches. Look, I tried my best and I lost. I'm human, I cannot play good every day. But there was no war, no one was killed. It was just a tennis match."

Yet, most would agree that you cannot ascribe the tenets of professional sports to the minors. It would be a little like comparing the responsibilities of the chief executive officer of Coca Cola to those of a child and her lemonade stand.

The importance of most decisions depends entirely on perspective.

Every parent knows that little Erica isn't going to get rich from selling lemonade to passers-by on the curb, but she's learning valuable life lessons. Try telling the CEO of Coca Cola it isn't important if he shows a profit this year as long as he is honest and diligent in his work. That's one conversation I'd love to overhear.

The same understanding must be applied to sports. By their very definition, professional sports are about money and profit, and only indirectly about athletics and fun. Vince Lombardi, coach of the Super Bowl winning Green Bay Packers once said, "Winning isn't everything, it's the only thing." He can be forgiven for his delusion by bearing in mind that the stakes are high in the majors. A professional coach worries about his reputation for winning or creating winners because that ability directly affects his income potential as a professional coach. Billions of dollars are at play here, so it is fair to say that this is a horse of a different colour. Coaches at that level are certainly not out there to teach professional athletes important lessons about life values. The chasm between coaching professionals and coaching children is wide and deep!

In the following chapters we are going to take a look at the definition of each lesson children ought to learn through minor sports. They are worth examining in order to set a standard for interpretation and preclude ambiguity— to create a yard-stick, if you will.

I can't think of a better way to set a gauge than by introducing you to Coach Eddie. He is not someone I made up— he is as real as you and me. He has coached children's teams in a variety of sports and for over twenty years. But don't look to Coach Eddie as our model coach. In fact, he is quite the opposite, and stands as an example of part of what is wrong within minor sports. Coach Eddie applies the rules of professional sports to little league, believing that you must win at all costs. But don't judge him too harshly, lest you recognize him in the mirror. Remember that Coach Eddie is doing what he sincerely believes is right. Unfortunately, he has lost his perspective.

FOR PARENTS AND COACHES

Compare your list of what you think coaches should be teaching with the list provided in the above chapter. Add new items from this list to your list that you find appropriate. As you go through this book, note the things that are being taught well in your sports organization. Mark the areas where questions are raised and problems exist. This will create a good list of areas that need improvement. Each precept in the next twenty chapters is followed by questions and suggestions to aid in your assessment of how well the organization, as well as individual coaches, are doing in these important areas.

VI: FIRST PRECEPT—
SPORTSMANSHIP

"Young men soon give and soon forget affronts." — *Addison*

Clearly, sportsmanship is the number-one response from parents and coaches when addressing the lessons learned through minor sports. What exactly is sportsmanship? Why do most people feel this is what coaches should be teaching children? Just how important is it?

The dictionary defines sportsmanship as fair-mindedness. Essentially, this means applying the rules equally to all players, and maintaining perspective. It means being a good winner as well as a good loser. A win is not something to gloat over, because although you won this time, it is inevitable that, at some time, you will lose. Knowing and understanding this will help you to win graciously.

Being a gracious winner is part of the positive attitude

that you must pass on to the kids on your team. It is your job to create an environment of positive learning, not one in which the child is afraid to make a mistake. Always remember that the emotional state of a child is a very fragile thing. Children who are not afraid to make mistakes have a significant advantage, whereas those who are taught through a punishment system of doing push-ups, running around the field, skating around the rink, sitting on the bench, will drown in a pool of insecurity. If you destroy a child's desire to try new skills by belittling his achievements, you are an autocrat with an ego that has no place in little league.

As children learn new skills, they thrill in the process itself. Their self-esteem comes from doing the best they possibly can, not from your perception of perfection. You must encourage the effort, not necessarily the action.

The antithesis of winning, is, of course, losing. If *you* have never been taught how to lose, you won't be prepared to teach children how to lose. It doesn't have to be hard, and it certainly needn't be traumatic. Losing should simply be looked upon as a passing experience in life. One that has nothing to do with self-worth! You were there, you played the game, you still have the experience. You may have the flip-side, but you still have the coin.

Losing is one of those lessons that must have passed Coach Eddie by. One day his team was winning by one run. When his centre fielder dropped a fly-ball, it resulted in a tie game. Coach Eddie went ballistic the moment the ball hit the ground, almost as though he expected the kid to drop the ball— almost as though he expected failure. He screamed for the fielder to get his butt on the bench, while a teammate ran out to take his place. The boy— yes, just a boy— cowered on the bench while Coach Eddie convinced him of his worthlessness! Coach Eddie benched him. Coach Eddie screamed at him. Coach Eddie humiliated him in front of his teammates and his parents sitting in the stands. What must have been going through the mind of that child as he sat trembling on the bench? He had dropped a ball! Did that really warrant malevolence? Children will naturally shun negative experiences, and Coach Eddie's centre fielder never returned to the field.

The following is a letter I received from Dan, in Seattle, Washington.

When I was in the seventh grade I went out for little league baseball. The coach of the team saw his role like that of a major league manager. His job was to win. Since we had recently moved, the coach didn't know who I was or what I could do, so I sat on the bench for three straight games. At each of the three games my father asked when I would get to play and reminded the coach about the purpose of little league ball. Each time he was told I would get to play soon.

During the fourth game my father confronted the coach near the end of the game and demanded I be put in the game. There was a strong atmosphere of physical threat in the confrontation. The coach snarled and put me in the game. Since everyone present had witnessed the altercation, I was the centre of attention. All conversation stopped and every eye was on me as I stood terrified at the plate. I struck out on the first three pitches and immediately quit the team. As things turned out, I was a very good athlete and I love baseball. However, I never played ball again. I'm in my late forties now and have always regretted the baseball I never got to play because of this one incident.

Dan's trauma is over thirty years old, yet even in his late forties he still remembers the humiliation as though it were yesterday. One very misguided coach directly affected the life of another human being by losing sight of sportsmanship.

If you see a little of Coach Eddie in the way you coach, it's time to adjust. Sportsmanship is the number-one choice of what we should be teaching children as coaches. It's time to teach by example.

You lost— be a good sport about it.
You won— be a good sport about it.

The quality of behaviour of individuals in both victory and defeat is what sportsmanship is all about. In any sport, as in life, mistakes are inevitable. To accept this is to understand that a person's value is not determined by his accomplishments on the field. To the truly sportsmanlike individual, mistakes are learning experiences. Properly handled, this message will be passed along to the children.

In effect, when you create an environment of sportsmanship, you are giving your charges a perspective awareness.

They will know how to win well, to lose well, and to remember, above all, that it is a game, a diversion, a way to have fun!

FOR PARENTS AND COACHES: SPORTSMANSHIP

Do you believe sportsmanship is being promoted in your sports organization? Consider how parents, coaches, and children react to mistakes, errors, game losses and game wins. Do children mock each other after games? Are humiliation and abuse tolerated?

VII: SECOND PRECEPT—
PHYSICAL SKILL

"The dwarf sees farther than the giant, when he has the giant's shoulders to mount on." — *Coleridge*

The human body is truly a remarkable piece of work, both in repose but especially in action. Our bodies can bend, jump, twist, turn, run, and roll. We were made for physical movement. In fact, our very health, mental and physical, is directly linked to exercise. Evidence suggests that our self-image is dependent upon participation in some kind of physical activity.

Millions of Canadians participate in daily physical activities such as swimming, running, walking, tennis, golf, aerobics, soccer, softball, bowling, cycling, hockey— the list is as long as your imagination. Naturally, we all participate at different levels and to a greater or lesser extent, yet each of us is capable of performing certain physical skills and attempting new ones. It isn't important if we play hockey like Wayne Gretzkey, or golf like Greg Norman. It is important only that we perform each task to the best of our ability, even if the end result is only adequate. Children who are trying to learn new skills need to hear: "Good catch," "Great try," "That's wonderful," "Boy, you sure are improving," "Look at you!" It's entirely possible that it isn't wonderful, that he isn't improving, that it wasn't a great catch. But each effort is a great try, because it is in the nature of every healthy child to strive with enormous effort.

Most parents understand the need for children to be active, and this is evidenced by the millions involved in minor sports. Yet somewhere along the way we've lost sight of the importance of participation and replaced it with the importance of winning. Imagine the following conversation between a parent and coach.

"How did the team do today?"

"The team did great! We practised all week long how to place the feet when trying to bunt. During the game each child stood perfectly. I'm so proud of them. We really learned something today. It's a great feeling. It's what keeps me coaching."

"But did we win?"

"You know, I'm not really sure. I'm so pleased that the kids learned to bunt so well, I never even thought of whether we won or lost the game."

It is wonderful to encounter a coach so wrapped up in a child's development that he doesn't recall the score of the game, and this is remarkable when you look at it from the eyes of the children. They have been taught, encouraged, and praised for their efforts, rather than for winning the game. Whether they win or lose becomes irrelevant. They are having fun!

As it turns out, that was a real conversation held between Wayne, a coach of ten-year-olds, and me. I was talking with a coach whose philosophy was to teach and sharpen physical skills with little focus on the outcome of each game. This caused me to wonder just how much emphasis should be placed on winning and, further, what the effect was on the children he coached.

My curiosity was soon satisfied. A year later, when registration came around, each child who had been coached by Wayne made a special notation on their registration form. It read, "Please put me on Wayne's team!" I believe this is where the prosecution says, "I rest my case."

I followed Wayne's coaching that year. At all of his practices, the emphasis was on developing new skills. Players whose physical abilities were good helped those who needed a little extra practice. The only thing required was for each child to try to the best of his ability. At games the players put these new skills to work. They all got equal game time and each was encouraged to "shoot for the impossible." They knew there would be no punishment here for mistakes. They were fearless in their determination, their support for one another was unconditional, and they played with absolute delight.

Unfortunately, coaches like Wayne are a rare breed. Too many are like Coach Eddie. He uses his average players only as much as the rules dictate he must, preferring, instead, to play his "stars." His object is to win at any or all costs. Those costs are the self-confidence, self-esteem, enthusiasm and general strength of character of the children on his team.

I compared Coach Eddie's instruction that year to Wayne's. A typical practice saw Eddie pick his four best players and put them in the infield. For nearly an hour Coach Eddie hit ball after ball to each of his luminaries, practising every conceivable variation on an infield play in preparation for the next game they would win. Errors were not tolerated.

The rest of the team was ushered to the outfield where parents who happened to be on hand hit fly balls to them. Worse than negative attention, Coach Eddie paid those children no attention at all.

As a parent, I am ultimately responsible for the well-being of my children. I know which coach I would choose.

Teaching physical skills is not about how fast you can run. It's not about how high you can jump. It is about executing bodily movement to produce maximum efficiency. There is a difference between physical dominance and developing physical skill. The coach's job is to assess the physical ability of each of his players, to encourage them to push those limits and, finally, to accept their best, whatever that may be.

"They are able— because they think they are able," wrote Virgil.

FOR PARENTS AND COACHES: PHYSICAL SKILL

Consider whether the physical skills of individual children are being improved and made an important part of practices and games. Are the children equally encouraged and provided with appropriate and useful practice tasks? Does your organization have age-appropriate skills improvement plans that are simple and fun to institute?

VIII: THIRD PRECEPT—
TEAMWORK

*"No man can be provident of his time who is not
prudent in the choice of his company."* — *Jeremy Taylor*

Teamwork is a unique phenomenon in that the more players
who display it, the better the team will perform. It results
when individuals set aside their personal aspirations for the
good of the whole. When it works, each member becomes
aware that his best interest is served by helping the others on
his team to achieve a common outcome.

The coach's job— your job— is to teach children that
the team is not dependent upon a single individual to win the
game any more than it is the fault of a single individual if you
lose a game. What good is the gifted athlete with no teammates? Imagine a soccer match with a full team complement

faced-off against an opposing team with just one player! It seems ludicrous to picture that scenario, but no more so than allowing any one team member to consider himself a "star," and thus, indispensable.

That's not to say that certain athletes don't sometimes dominate a game due to superior physical size, strength or co-ordination, but even those individuals must learn to perform within the framework of the team. A single player cannot possibly win a game alone and, inevitably, the day will come when your 'star' will compete with others who are just as good, or better, than he is.

Even Coach Eddie knows this. Unfortunately, he is one of those who believes that a single individual can be blamed for a loss. His solution to this imaginary problem is to bench perceived inferior players as much as possible. Whether deliberate or not, he is sending the message that not playing helps the team. What does that teach children about team-work, and what will it do to their self-confidence?

I recall one year in which Coach Eddie acquired a particularly gifted pitcher, Jim, whose abilities far surpassed the average for house league. Needless to say, Jim threw one shutout after another, striking out most batters that faced him. Coach Eddie used Jim in every game, in every inning. During one game, with the score standing at 15 to 0, the opposing team's coach asked Coach Eddie to replace Jim so his team could get a few runs and have some fun, as the win was already assured. He refused. "You coach your team and I'll coach mine!" was his reply. I wonder what Coach Eddie's team learned about teamwork that year?

I can only guess what his reasons were, but Jim never played again after that year.

The concept of teamwork doesn't just apply to sports. It's a lesson we carry with us into our personal lives as well, whether at work or within our communities. If our children learn to understand and work within the group dynamic at a young age, they will be masters of collaboration in their adult lives. Our children will reap the many benefits of teamwork, among them the comfort of peer approval, the satisfaction that comes from feeling part of a group, and the delight of working towards a common goal. We are, after all, social creatures, who crave the company of others.

FOR PARENTS AND COACHES: TEAMWORK

Are coaches and parents playing favourites? Are they making sure that all children work together, appreciate their own and each other's contributions to their mutual efforts, and that all children share in the joy of team accomplishments? Is each child made to feel that he or she belongs? Are teams also rewarded for effort?

IX: FOURTH PRECEPT—
LEARNING THE GAME

"...live to learn..." — *Bayard Taylor*

"The real character of a man is found out by his amusement."
— *Sir Joshua Reynolds*

Unfortunately, little league activities are one hundred percent dependent upon volunteers. Fortunately, there are a great many who do volunteer.

It's easy to judge a situation from the outside, but only when you become personally involved as a volunteer do you realize the enormous amount of dedication required. There are times when you wonder if it's worth the effort.

Yes, it certainly is worth it, especially when you remember who you're volunteering for. As a volunteer in little league, you must rise above controversies and confrontations, and stay focused on individual, as well as team, goals. But first, be certain what those goals are. Certainly, improving physical skills is one. The year my son's team needed a coach or we'd lose the season a wonderful thing happened. The father of one of the boys volunteered, although he knew nothing about the rules of soccer. Consequently, his focus was on having fun, not winning or losing, which didn't matter at all to the children. Each budding Pele had a chance to kick the ball, giving Mom and Dad temporary bragging rights. Everybody had fun, parents and children alike, with no thought to league standing.

Remember, a skill learned is a success, even if only

Mom! Dad! Did you see me? I kicked it!

performed adequately. How vividly I remember one little boy, Christopher, who had been trying to master a kick, that elusive foot-meets-ball skill that adults take for granted. When finally, to his own astonishment, his size four shoe made contact with that black and white sphere, nothing could hide his elation! He ran to Mom and Dad, jumping up and down, shouting, "Did you see me? I kicked it!" No matter that the ball didn't go anywhere. This was a skill learned that created visions of greatness in that little boy's mind's eye, and ear-to-ear beams for his parents.

All that season our father-turned-coach read books on soccer and coaching techniques, and together he and his team learned about the game. But they never lost sight of the truly important goal of having fun.

Of course, the more coaches know about the game and how to teach the skills of playing it, the better, especially with older players. A good coach will concentrate on developing new skills into habits. Repeating a certain skill and verbally encouraging its progress ensures that that skill becomes a habit. It doesn't take long for the astute athlete to figure out that this habit brings about success more times than not, and so this habit becomes second-nature to him— routine, if you like. As each learned skill becomes routine, the coach takes the player to the next level of skill. As in any skill a child learns, the whole process is best accomplished with encouragement rather than punishment. Contrary to what many coaches think, children do not respond well to loud, bullying instruction. They become frightened and nervous when they know the coach will punish them if they don't get it right.

To get the very best out of a child try a little honey— because vinegar stings.

Darin, from Hampton, Virginia, writes:

Due to negative events when I was nine years old and on a baseball team, I never played organized sports again. That's over twenty years ago. I have a son now, Austin, who is nine years old and in the third grade. When Austin was in kindergarten, he brought home a sign-up sheet for T-ball. I thought it would be fun for him to have opportunities that I never had, so we signed him up. We were told that we would be contacted by a coach in early March. Midway through April I contacted the youth club office to advise that we hadn't been contacted by a coach. I was told, 'Uh, we haven't found a coach for your son's team. Would you be willing to coach?' My son was in the same room, as I replied, 'I don't know anything about baseball, so I couldn't possibly be a coach.' Austin jumped up and down begging, 'Say yes, Dad, please, please, please.'

Three days later I found myself out on a grassy field, surrounded by ten five-year-olds, nervously wondering how I got myself into this situation. I started the practice by asking where they would find first base. My first surprise! I was the only one who knew.

Six out of the original ten children will be starting a fourth season with me this year. I guess I'll stay in it as long as I still know one thing more than they do, and as long as they are having fun. I didn't realize how much they looked up to me until I overheard one day, as a group of them were car-pooling home from a practice, one child declared, 'And Austin gets to go home with him!'"

Darin is a coach who has his goals straight. He says he'll be coaching as long as he knows one thing more than the kids, and as long as they are still having fun.

For the sake of the children, let's hope Darin stays in it a long time.

FOR PARENTS AND COACHES: LEARNING THE GAME

Are practices broken down into age-appropriate and skill-developing areas? Are practices enjoyable, full of learning and fun? Is practice kept within reasonable limits in terms of the age group and desire of the children? Is the game being taught in a clear, logically expanding and understandable way?

X: FIFTH PRECEPT—
BEING FAIR

"One man's word is no man's word;
we should quietly hear both sides." — *Goethe*

"There are no judgements so harsh as those of the erring, the
inexperienced, and the young." — *Mulock*

lack of fairness

Today's child, if surrounded by fairness, is tomorrow's adult
who upholds justice.

A truly fair situation can only be achieved through
objective eyes, and that is, perhaps, the most difficult part of
being human. We can't always see things through unbiased
eyes because we are subjective beings. We base our opinions,
our judgements and our actions on our own perspective—
as we see things. Perception affects reality.

When Coach Eddie was asked to replace his unstoppable

pitcher, Jim, in a mercy situation, he refused. In his eyes, his decision was the right one. He had a star pitcher and he would use him. Period. To Coach Eddie, fairness was not an issue, not even a consideration. So, Jim continued to pitch every inning, and the game was a bore to watch and to play— no one had fun. But Coach Eddie got to be the hero because his team "slaughtered" the other team. Of course, it didn't occur to him that he was a hero in his eyes only.

As a coach, one of your greatest challenges is to be fair. What would you do if you found yourself, one season, with an outstanding talent on your team? The intoxicating temptation is to use that athlete every chance you get. To show him off as though this incredible talent were somehow your doing.

There is no denying that talent like Jim's needs to be addressed and developed, providing, of course, that this is what Jim wants for himself. I would be remiss if I didn't point out the pitfalls of allowing the overzealous involvement of parents and coaches, which can destroy the psyche of a child. What seems like a simple game can become a deadly serious business when the adults involved see visions of fame and financial security.

The question remains, however, as to Jim's options, one being to join an all-star team. If he decides he wants to stay in house league his choices are to be used no more or less often than the other pitchers on the team, or to move up to the next age level division. This would have to be an executive level decision and, in the interests of fairness, would probably be the best one. On the one hand, Jim has every right to play in house league. On the other hand, there are some one-hundred-plus children who have the right to expect equal playing time. Parents come out to games expecting to take pleasure in watching the development of their own children. What joy can come of watching your child in a powerless situation, obviously out-matched by a super talent?

Several years ago, in Brantford, Ontario, there was a young hockey talent. His skill was so superior that he played in a higher age division for most of his youthful career. This kept his skills challenged and created a fair situation all around. Over the years I've enjoyed watching this young man develop into one of the best hockey players of all time. Of course I'm talking about Wayne Gretzky.

What if Gretzky had been forced to play at his own age level? Worse still, what if there had been a Coach Eddie in his life? Like Jim, he might have lost interest in the game and quit playing forever!

Too often, those young athletes with superior physical skills receive more attention from their coaches and get more playing time than those less skilled. But let me say again, that's not what house league is supposed to be about. As a minor sports coach, you are meant to give each team member equal opportunity to develop his athletic potential. If you still disagree, then you need to reassess your own motivation for being a little league coach.

FOR PARENTS AND COACHES: BEING FAIR

Are all children being given equal playing time and encouragement to improve? Are all children urged to do their best? Are disputes resolved fairly and in children's best interests, or are adult politics affecting the children? Is fairness part of the organization's mandate and rules?

XI: SIXTH PRECEPT—

HAVING FUN

"If those who are the enemies of innocent amusements had the direction of the world, they would take away the spring, and youth, the former from the year, the latter from human life."
— *Balzac*

This is the chapter to pay attention to above all the others, because it talks about having fun, that wonderful medium through which all lessons can be learned. It is part of the natural make-up of all children to want to have fun, motivating them to read, paint, listen to music, watch a movie, and, yes, play a game. When guiding a child toward a certain goal, your aim must be to create enthusiasm, rather than anxiety, because an anxious child learns nothing.

Think back to when you were in school getting ready to write an exam, or read aloud in class, or run the two-hundred metre dash. Chances are you were nervous, which caused untold misery, physically and mentally. You simply cannot function optimally when your body is trembling, it feels like your muscles have turned to mush, and your thinking process seems to have shut down. A coach's bullying can cause all of these things in youngsters not experienced enough to turn nervous energy into performance. Encourage *effort*, not out-come.

This philosophy is stated poignantly by a teenaged referee whose frustration caused her to write this letter to the editor.

'Christopher!' A woman screeches. 'Christopher! Get a move on it!'

'Christopher!' Another voice. 'Go for the ball!'

Christopher's head swivels as he listens first to his mother, then to his soccer coach, unsure of whose instructions to follow. He knows he should listen to the coach, but dreads the ride home if he ignores the shrill voice of his parent. He decides to pretend he hasn't heard either of them, and kicks the ball out of bounds.

The teenage referee calls a corner kick for the other team. Both mother and coach now shift their anger to the referee, who follows the boy's example and ignores them.

It's not easy for either the boy or the referee to ignore the shouted insults and criticism from adult spectators. Referees, like me, mutter all the smart comebacks and crushing answers we can think of... thoughts we know we can never say aloud, for to do so would be to reduce our authority and dignity to the level of the parent.

For adult referees, it's an unpleasant, but routine, part of the job. But for youth referees the constant condemnation is unsettling and demoralizing, not to mention personally wounding.

I will always remember the time when, at fourteen, in my first year of refereeing, a coach yelled at me for five minutes for accidentally cutting two minutes off an unimportant game.

Then, there was the time when I was running lines and a parent stood just behind me, criticizing every call I made against his team, softly enough that only I could hear. When I called the centre referee over to instruct this man to leave, he denied saying anything. Furthermore, the other spectators became angry when we insisted that he leave.

Officials of minor sports, whether referees or umpires, are people whose imperfections and minor mistakes are regularly met with abuse and insults that would be considered unacceptable in any other situation. I have been told to 'get glasses, stay home,' and asked, 'what's a girl doing on the field?' I have been called names and been sworn at.

The worst part is, you can't yell back. The parents are already setting a bad enough example for the kids. The referees, at least, have to be cool and professional. That's a lot to ask of an uncertain, insecure teenager.

Refereeing would be fun if it weren't for the adults. While there's the odd player who follows the example of the spectators and coaches, most of the kids are pleasant and co-operative. They will chat with you, tease you, and if you make a mistake they will let you know in a way that isn't *personally insulting or rude. Many parents get overly involved in minor sports because they see themselves in their children. As one woman commented to Christopher's mother, 'We want to win more than they do!'*

I wonder if those belligerent, determined parents will still see themselves in their children when those children become belligerent, determined teenagers who defy authority and swear when they don't get their way?

David versus Goliath. Fear versus arrogance. Honestly, who is having fun?

Our behaviour as adults— the example we are meant to set— and its direct effect on young, yet undeveloped, minds, is summed up eloquently in the last paragraph of this young referee's letter:

> *I wonder if those belligerent, determined parents will still see themselves in their children when those children become belligerent, determined teenagers who defy authority and swear when they don't get their way?"*

Thoreau wrote, "It takes two to speak the truth — one to speak, and another to hear." Are we listening?

Recently, a friend of mine recounted this experience from her own son's life, by way of support of the philosophies contained in this book.

> *When George was in elementary school, each day he would come home and get on the telephone to 'round up the guys' for a game of scrub, or whatever other sport they decided to play that day. I was often amazed at how much discussion went on over specific points within the rules— rules that they would bend at liberty based on how many came out to play and the calibre of play for the day.*
>
> *Occasionally, events erupted into an argument, but I found that, by and large, left on their own, they would play happily for hours, day after day after day. They must have been having fun or they wouldn't have carried on. In fact, I loved it when they played street hockey right outside my*

house because they laughed and cheered endlessly. They sounded like children are supposed to sound.

When George would finally come in after these pick-up games, he was always in a great mood, bubbling on and on to me about every last detail of the game. If I asked which team won he would look at me curiously, as if I had asked a really stupid question. Why? Because it didn't matter. What counted to these kids was their own performance as it related to a particular assist, save, shot, and so on.

George is now almost seventeen-years-old and he and his friends still play pick-up. The sport still varies, the rules still vary, yet what is unchanged is their delight.

Why, then, is winning so important to adults? That is not a simple question, and the answer is equally complicated. Average parents will probably tell you that they want their child to be successful and that means winning. A coach might feel that there's no point putting a team together if it isn't going to win. By now you should see that these answers lack perspective. They have little to do with the needs of children and more to do with egos of adults.

Sports psychologist Dr. Eric Margenau believes that the explanation lies in the insecurities of adults. He states:

The key element for parents to recognize is that a parent's desires can be, and often are, a function of his or her own lack of self-esteem and need to live vicariously and experience excellence through the performance of the child.

*The parent who feels secure, competent, and adequate
in the world isn't going to do that to a child.*

In the surveys that I conducted, when I asked what
children should be learning, the number-one response was
sportsmanship. Having fun was number six. Yet, when
children up to age fifteen were asked the same question, their
number-one response was having fun!

We take a game— a diversion for amusement— we
organize it, we add rules, we change rules, we bring in
coaches, we bring in arbiters, we keep track of the score. But
do we make it better?! The fact of the matter is that when
we involve ourselves in the play of children, we don't always
make things better.

If you want to coach children in a meaningful way that
will have a positive impact on their lives, then you must
remember to maintain a proper perspective. Put as much fun
into your coaching as you possibly can. It's the fun the
children will remember long after the score is forgotten.

FOR PARENTS AND COACHES: HAVING FUN

Consider whether rewards or negative reinforcements
are being used regularly with the children. What kinds of
negative reinforcement are being tolerated? Should they
be? What kinds of rewards are provided to the children?
Are the children taught to seek for nothing but the
abstract gleam of a trophy off in the distance— with

nothing for the teams that don't "win" at the end of the season or tournament? Or are children taught to enjoy their own development, their own accomplishments, their team advances in combining skills as the season goes along, and rewarded for that hard work and for trying their best? Is time for fun built into practices?

XII: SEVENTH PRECEPT—
DISCIPLINE AND SELF-CONTROL

"You cannot teach a man anything;
you can only help him to find it within himself." — *Galileo*

A twelve-year-old is racing toward the goal, soccer ball at his feet. With mounting excitement at the thrill of his impending third goal playing in his mind, he is tripped by an opposing player. No penalty is called— the ref has missed it. The twelve-year-old gets up and angrily kicks the ball, swearing at the defending player. A scuffle breaks out, and, because he initiated the fight, he is ejected from the game. His team loses. The coach, teammates and parents are upset with the referee. They scream and swear at him— they don't know it's his birthday.

Sadly, anger is all they'll all take away with them from

that game. The referee missed a tripping call. Officials at all levels miss calls and they always will. Somewhere along the way that twelve-year-old learned to channel his frustration into violence. Fighting is a learned behaviour and we need to look to our own conduct as the source. If we don't teach self-discipline by example, how can we expect it of our children or those we guide?

When I spoke to the young official after that game, he admitted that he missed the call, and he felt terrible about it. Yet he couldn't understand why the adults were so rude to him. Unfortunately, I couldn't explain it either, but I assured him their behaviour was inappropriate.

Coach Eddie would not have found the actions of the coach, or the spectators, or even the player, out of place under the circumstances. He believes he knows all about discipline. If you make a mistake on Coach Eddie's team, you do ten push-ups. If you make the same mistake again, you run laps around the field. If you don't live up to his expectations, you'll find yourself getting splinters on the bench.

Someone once asked Coach Eddie why he benched a player who had struck out. He replied, "When I was a kid that's how my coach disciplined me when I struck out. It worked, because I still remember it. The kid will never forget, will he?"

And he is absolutely right. That child will never forget. It won't improve his batting, and he'll face the next at-bat with fear of failure, but he surely won't forget. The fact is, if you look at the incident, there isn't a single positive lesson to be learned from Coach Eddie's methods. All he is offering is negative reinforcement.

Most adults can remember a time from their childhood where the punishment is remembered long after the perceived infraction has been forgotten. It lies to every coach to ask himself what kind of influence he has on the kids.

Ryan, from Spokane, Washington, writes:

> *During spring and summer while growing up in the late fifties, I used to play baseball with the neighbourhood kids. We played in back yards and vacant lots. We'd pretended we were Mickey Mantle, Sandy Koufax or Willie Mays, cheered by thousands of fans in the make-believe stadium.*
>
> *During the eighth grade I looked forward to the coming baseball season. This would be my first opportunity to play on a real team. What a thrill it was to receive a T-shirt with my school name and a cap with the school colours and letter. I wasn't particularly strong or co-ordinated at that age, but I was there for every practice and tried my hardest. I don't recall the coach working with me to improve my skills and technique as he did with the other kids who had potential. I was there for every game, hoping for my chance to play.*
>
> *Finally, the last game of the season came and I was there, hopeful, as ever, that I'd get to play. Each inning my heart would race, hoping and praying the coach would call my name. He never did. I don't recall if we won that final game. I can't recall if we even won any games. What I do remember is that I never got a chance to play.*

My mom picked me up after that final game and I simply couldn't control the tears. That was the first time I told her that I hadn't played at all, the entire season.

I neither played nor attended a baseball game or any other sporting event for over twenty years.

If you still think your coaching isn't directly affecting the lives of the children on your team, please read Ryan's letter again. Each letter I receive is the story of person— a human being like you or me. Each one has a face and a name. These individuals have had value judgements made about them based on a coach's perception of their physical prowess. There is no greater folly!

I often ask coaches their reason for volunteering. Some say they believe they have something to teach the children. Others believe they are performing a community service. Still others coach because a son or daughter is on the team. There are likely as many reasons as there are coaches, yet one common thread binds all of these individuals— the responsibility to set the best possible example as a figure of authority in those children's lives. In your hands you hold their well-being. Children need to be spoken to in a positive manner, yet, as I go from event to event I hear more negative reinforcement than one would believe.

"If you mess up, we'll lose the game."
"That mistake could cost us the game."
"Don't blow it now."

"We don't want to be losers, do we?"

"Show them no mercy!"

"Don't you ever listen?!"

You've heard them, too, I know. You might even have used one or two in your coaching. Try to imagine if your employer spoke to you that way each day. Would it motivate you to work harder? To improve? Would it encourage you to like your boss and respect him? Most importantly, would it make you feel good about yourself? What goes through the mind of a child when he hears negative statements again and again? One player is no more responsible for losing a game than one individual was for starting World War II, or for Ford having to recall millions of vehicles due to a faulty ignition starter, or for Team Canada not getting Hockey Gold in the 1996 Winter Olympics.

Discipline is not about anger and punishment. It is about training the mind and developing character. It must come from within the individual. Learning to control temper, and the inner strength to rise above difficulties, these are what discipline is about. Work as a positive unit, encouraging each other as you strive for a common goal, and set the best example you can. That's how to teach self-control and achieve discipline.

FOR PARENTS AND COACHES: DISCIPLINE AND SELF-CONTROL

What kinds of lessons about discipline and self-control are evident in the role models— the parents and coaches— in your organization? Are children being taught to control their tempers while expressing legitimate frustration in a civilized way? Is collaborative dispute resolution part of your organization's usual operation?

XIII: EIGHTH PRECEPT—
MOTIVATION

"Selfishness is the grand moving principle of nine-tenths of our actions." — *La Rochefoucauld*

Motivation— simple in explanation, complex in execution. It is a factor that causes you to want to do a thing. Yet to motivate others can be difficult. How do you prompt the resolve to accomplish a certain task? By creating a desire to act. So easy to say, so hard to do. Or is it? Not if you remember that something that is pleasurable creates a natural desire to repeat it. *Wanting to* is the motivation!

The question is how to make children want to try their best, learn new skills, and go that extra mile. First let me give you an example of how to destroy those desires in children.

Coach Eddie forces team members who make a mistake to apologize to teammates. To further drive home his point, he benches the offender. This kind of action instils fear and resentment. I assure you, those are not motivators.

Children should never leave a game thinking that they caused their team to lose, or that they are not integral to the team. If your coaching is not emphasizing activity and participation, your motivational skills need some work. Before you can begin to inspire children to surpass even their own expectations, you must first get your own house in order. Ask yourself why you're coaching, and if you're having

...he can sit on the bench for the rest of the year for all I care...

a positive effect on those children. If, in all good conscience, you believe you are, then you, too, must believe that winning has nothing to do with winning. Choose not to be a coach who does more long-term damage than good. Set realistic individual goals, discuss team goals, and you will be on your way to the right motivation. I cannot stress enough the need to emphasize having fun, because having fun is what will keep the children motivated.

FOR PARENTS AND COACHES: MOTIVATION

Is effort rewarded and recognized? Is a calm and supportive atmosphere provided for the children? Are all children included and encouraged?

XIV: NINTH PRECEPT—
HOW TO WIN

"It is the contest that delights us, and not the victory."
— *Pascal*

On the surface it seems winning isn't something you need to think about— you just do it. Coach Eddie certainly knows how to win. He uses his best players as much as the rules allow, while less-skilled children play little or not at all. Years ago, Coach Eddie had to deal with new rules which stipulated that each child must play in a minimum of two innings. He figured out a way to abide by the rules and still play the game his way. He put team players with lesser skill in for *one pitch* and then pulled them. With tears welling they would ask to be put back in the game, only to be told "go home and don't come back until you grow up!" Some never did come back. They probably decided that being on a winning team wasn't enough— they wanted to play, to feel part of that team. Coach Eddie won the championship that year. He got another trophy to gather dust on the mantel.

When normal, healthy, developing children are put in a situation where the only absolute is to win, they become anxious, and an anxious child cannot function normally; in fact, such a child cannot develop normally. Given the choice, most children will walk away from a situation that makes them feel bad about themselves. Contrary to what some believe, toughing it out with a verbally abusive coach will not build character. It can lead to loss of sleep or appetite, or the child might develop physical ailments brought on by stress. We acknowledge the evils of stress in adulthood:

irritability, high blood pressure, risk of stroke or heart attack, or general depression. It is no less damaging to a child, and maybe even more so. I quote again from Dr. Eric Margenau: "When the emphasis is placed solely on winning or advancing, most of the healthy aspects of athletics are lost."

Winning is not hard to do— winning graciously is. Firstly, it is important to insist that no one belittles any member of the opposing team. Then you should remind your team that a win today is nice, but there are no guarantees for the next time.

Naturally, every parent wants his or her child to be a winner, but whether or not this is a good thing depends on your definition of winning. The dictionary gives us a variety to choose from:

- *To be victorious in a battle, game or race.*
- *To obtain or achieve as the result of a battle or contest or bet.*
- *To obtain as a result of effort or perseverance.*
- *To gain the favour or support of.*
- *To succeed after a struggle in reaching a certain state or place.*

As a parent, a coach, a teacher— a role model— it is your responsibility to help a child develop skills, self-esteem, self-confidence and self-discipline. It is not in your job description to put your ego above the needs of the children.

FOR PARENTS AND COACHES: HOW TO WIN

Is success after a struggle and achievement your definition of winning, whether that struggle is to learn a simple, seemingly obvious skill or something larger? Are the children being taught to win graciously, appreciating their opponents' efforts?

XV: TENTH PRECEPT—
LEADERSHIP

"I am not a teacher: only a fellow-traveller of whom you asked the way. I pointed ahead— ahead of myself as well as of you." — *George Bernard Shaw*

Leadership can easily be defined as the ability to guide others. That makes us all leaders. As parents, teachers, aunts, uncles, singers, actors, radio announcers, sports heroes, and, of course, little league coaches, we all touch the lives of children on a daily basis. Therefore, it is important to think about the different kinds of leadership and what children respond to best. The first place to start is, naturally, by setting the best possible example, as we've already discussed. Children exemplify the saying "monkey see, monkey do."

I turn, once again, to Coach Eddie, who is my perfect example of how not to coach children. During a championship tournament the situation was a "must win" for both teams: one would advance and the other would be eliminated. Late in the game there were a couple of close calls at first base, 'and both were called outs. Predictably, Coach Eddie went berserk, screaming at the umpire. Following his lead the children then displayed their anger with a customary verbal barrage, including obscenities. The situation further degenerated with Coach Eddie and his team throwing equipment in disgust. Some of the children threw their hats to the ground and stomped on them. Some even threw themselves on the ground and cried. Coach Eddie was ejected. As he left the park, he screamed at the umpire, "See what you've done to the kids?"

Despite the well-respected reputation of the umpire and the indisputable fact that both calls were correct, albeit close, Coach Eddie's team accused the umpire of intentionally causing them to lose the game. This is another example of what the children learned from Coach Eddie.

The responsibilities of leadership don't begin and end with the coach. Parental leadership, too, is important at the games in which your child is participating. He may not get assists, goals, or hits, and he may make mistakes during the game. How are you going to handle it? What you say and what you do are just as important as how the coach responds. In fact, more so, because you are the constants in your child's life and he looks to you for unconditional support.

Similarly, the way in which you react to a perceived bad call sends a very clear message to your child. If you rant and rave and blame others, if you denigrate the official, then you have done harm by teaching a bad lesson. Children carry negative lessons with them throughout their lives. Fortunately, most parents take the ups and downs of the game in stride, not getting too upset over decisions made by umpires or referees, choosing, instead, to put the game into its proper perspective.

It's difficult, I know, to always be mindful of the example we are setting for the children around us, yet it is imperative. If you are coaching for the right reasons in the first place, then setting a good example and displaying proper leadership will be important to you.

FOR PARENTS AND COACHES: LEADERSHIP

Are coaches and parents leading by example, or is shouting and arbitrary imposition of will tolerated? Are lessons contradicted by adult actions? Is there consistency between lessons and verbal instructions to children and adult behaviour?

XVI: ELEVENTH PRECEPT—
HOW TO COMPETE

"None but yourself who are your greatest foe." — *Longfellow*

When we compete we are testing our skills in friendly rivalry. That's what amateur competition is all about. It is meant to be fun, exciting and, most importantly, leave us with fond memories.

How to compete is clearly the one thing that separates the major leagues from children's leagues. Coaches who apply professional-level techniques and aggression to children's' games must be made to see that this has no place in little league.

I offer two scenarios. The owner of a major league franchise is confronting his coach about their fifth straight loss. The coach explains, "It's not whether you win or lose, it's how you play the game." Chances are that coach isn't going to keep his job for very long.

The second scene is of parents confronting the coach of their children's team. They've also just lost their fifth straight game. The coach says, "It's not whether you win or lose, it's how you play the game."

These two examples may seem absurd at first glance, but think about the idea of competition in each case. In the first scenario, we're dealing with a multi-million dollar business. Every person involved, at every level, is an adult, and very much aware of how high the stakes are, yet they have chosen a path in life in which their value is based upon performance. It's not pretty, but the financial rewards can be huge.

Little league is about children, and the adults who volunteer to coach them must be prepared to be teachers as well. Winning at all costs must not be the motivation for competition. Young children don't care about winning and losing.

When little league coaches bend or break the rules, they are sending the message that they don't respect these rules. When they argue with game officials, employ intimidation tactics, or use illegal equipment, they are teaching children how to cheat. If your child is on a team where the coach uses these techniques of competition, you should ask yourself if that is really what you want your child to learn, and if not, make a point of voicing your concerns. You might wish to send a message to the executive, or attend an executive meeting. You could also get involved in coaching personally. That's the surest method I know to bring about change.

Coach Eddie encouraged children to use their size and momentum to run into defensive players, hoping for a dropped ball or to break up a double play. He encouraged them to "accidentally" kick the opponent covering a base so that the kicked child would fear being hurt again and shy away from the base on the next play. When they recapped after a game, the discussion was often about the pain they had inflicted and how it had made the intended victim cry. Coach Eddie taught his players to be mean-spirited. He called this healthy aggression, but let's not mince words. What was done was just plain mean, and that's not what we should be teaching children.

Fortunately, most coaches do play within the rules and they try to teach the kids what is, and what is not, appropriate behaviour. These coaches understand that everyone involved in minor sports is human— kids, coaches, parents, officials— and sometimes make mistakes. When children experience this kind of coaching they learn fair play. They are encouraged to do their best because that is all anyone can ask of us. It's all we can ask of ourselves. That's what little league competition is all about.

FOR PARENTS AND COACHES: HOW TO COMPETE

Are children being taught to compete with themselves, to improve at their own level and to do their best? Are children being taught to enjoy these successes, or are such successes ignored in favour of adult-oriented goals?

XVII: TWELFTH PRECEPT—
PHYSICAL FITNESS

"Man is of soul and body, formed for deeds...." — Shelley

What is fitness? How important is it? Is it physical or psychological?

Fitness is the state of being in suitable condition to do something, and that can be physical, mental, or both. Whether you are preparing for an exam in school, or for the decathlon, the more prepared you are, the better your chance to excel. Its importance is aptly described by James Michener in his book *Sports in America*:

> *I believe that children, like little animals, require play and competition in order to develop. I believe that play is a major agency in civilizing infants. I believe that big muscle movement helps the infant establish his balance within the*

space in which he will henceforth operate. I believe that competition, reasonably supervised, is essential to the full maturing of the individual.

Michener is not alone in his belief that each child must develop physically in order to obtain good health in mind and body. According to Dr. Eric Margenau, psychologists agree that movement of the muscles creates body awareness which leads to a sense of self-assurance and control.

Therefore, it is important to prepare children for a given task— game, race, etc.— to ensure that they don't incur injury and will be able to perform at their optimum. Regardless of physical abilities, pre-game callisthenics are essential. Small children certainly don't require the same warm-up period that adults do, but getting them used to the routine will develop a good life-long habit.

When we watch sporting events on television, we don't see the pre-game exercises that the athletes perform, so children are not aware that even their heroes exercise before each and every game. A child's natural exuberance pushes him to get right into the game with one hundred percent effort, but without proper warm-up they risk long-term injury which could plague them for the rest of their lives. A simple routine of exercises before each activity can prevent such injury.

It is the coach's job to encourage children to show up ten minutes early and stretch those little arms and legs. To that end, it's a good idea for each coach to familiarize himself with a variety of exercises associated with the game they're coaching. Libraries carry many books of this nature and there are also video tapes available on every sport. Most regions across the country hold coaching clinics which can be very helpful. In fact, it should be mandatory for any coach to attend these clinics.

Remember, it's not enough just to have the little ones run around the field a couple of times. While this is good for their cardiovascular health, it doesn't stretch specific muscles that they'll be using during the activity.

FOR PARENTS AND COACHES: PHYSICAL FITNESS

Are the children taught to warm up and cool down before and after strenuous activity? Is practice time dedicated to overall fitness of the children, including cardiovascular fitness, or is practice dedicated only to specific game skills? Is part of the goal of the children's work with their teams to gently improve fitness? Is fitness part of an overall strategy to keep injury to children to a minimum? Is fitness and health part of the mandate of your organization?

XVIII: THIRTEENTH PRECEPT—
PATIENCE

"He that can have patience can have what he will."
— *Franklin*

Teach children tolerance and they will grow up patient.

Patience. Every day of our lives things happen that test our patience, and each of us reacts differently. Think about your own degree of patience— it's crucial to your coaching— but it's difficult to assess.

Say you are driving along a two-way highway. The car in front of you is doing the posted speed limit, but you want to go faster. You think about passing. If you're a patient driver, you'll pass when it is safe to do so. If you are not, you'll pass at will, presuming it is safe. Which driver are you?

You're standing in a long line-up at the ATM, the theatre, a restaurant, the bank, or even the ice cream parlour.

Each person in that line will respond to the wait with varying degrees of patience. Some will take the wait in stride, talking and laughing the moments away, while others will become visibly agitated. They mumble, they grumble, and they annoy others around them. By the time their turn arrives, anger and frustration are in control. Which sort of person are you?

We all have our own comfort zone— and a pace that suits our personality, whether at work or play. Yet, now and then circumstances arise which force us to move either a little faster or a little slower. How we react is a test of our patience, our inner tranquillity. Children, too, have their own pace at which they do things, and some children learn more quickly than others.

In school, teachers often display an incredible amount of patience with students who take a little longer to grasp new concepts. It's something good teachers work very hard to develop, understanding its benefit to the students. A patient teacher knows she will experience success in the end, whereas one who is less patient will turn the lesson into an exercise in frustration for everyone involved.

Minor league coaches are also teachers. They, too, inter-act with children, teaching them new skills, and being the best role models they can be. Yet I've noticed a significant difference. When a school teacher has a student who is experiencing a particularly difficult time with some new skill, she will work longer and harder with that one student, even granting him extra time on her lunch hour, or after school, in order to help that child catch up. Conversely, when a coach experiences a similarly difficult situation, he too often mistakenly believes that he can bully that child into learning. Instead of patiently giving more of his time, he will impatiently cast that child aside as unable to succeed, or worse, cause him to believe that he simply isn't trying hard enough.

I have no time for mistakes. Hmph. Maybe if I bully him, he will quit the team...

Coach Eddie believes that coaching is very different from teaching. His desire to win leaves little room for tolerance. Coach Eddie is wrong, because he doesn't understand that winning isn't what it's about. The children are what it's about. They are little individuals whose bodies and minds are still developing. Boys and girls whose emotions run close to the surface, who are perceptively aware that coach doesn't treat each one the same. Little people who will be adults and will react to life using the tools they were given in childhood. What tools are you giving them?

Patience is a very special quality. With it a person has the capacity to endure pain, troubles or hardships without complaint. Patience gives us the ability to persevere without losing heart or becoming bored. How many of our own decisions would have been different if we'd just had a little more patience? How patient are you as a coach?

FOR PARENTS AND COACHES: PATIENCE

Is coaching in your organization impatient and easily frustrated with the sincere efforts of children? Are coaches kindly guides, or do they expect to behave like tyrants? Are children given the time they need to learn?

XIX: FOURTEENTH PRECEPT—
RESPECT

"A moral, sensible, and well-bred man
Will not affront me, and no other can." — Cowper

Within every person there is an extraordinary power. Most people live their entire lives and never realize the magic of that power, yet how one uses it might well determine one's destiny. It is so delicate a thing that a single negative incident can reduce that power to nothing. On the other hand, when used positively, it can move mountains.

That power is respect. Respect is not for sale, nor can you bully others into it, for, although many may defer to you, these polite displays are but ghosts of the real thing. How, then, do you gain the respect of others?

Coach Eddie believed that using fear of punishment

would achieve his ultimate goal— to win. He mistakenly believed that the more games he won, the greater would be the respect people paid him, and the children were mere pawns in his personal pursuit. Fear and intimidation were tools he used to mould the children into obedience. He probably believed he had their respect.

One particular year, Coach Eddie was without a pitcher, so he called a child-star who had not signed up and offered to pay him to play. Yes, Coach Eddie offered a cash incentive for each win and each shutout. Coach Eddie probably believed he could buy the pitcher's respect.

There is no magical formula for earning the respect of the kids on your team, although earning is a good place to start. Once again, I'm going to compare coaching to teaching, where some of the best examples are set. I recently had a discussion with an elementary school French teacher, Christina, who also helps coach the school sports teams before class, during her lunch hour, and after school. Her programs, both in and out of the classroom, are incredibly successful and her popularity with the students is almost legendary. I asked her how she earned such respect from her students.

It's not something I think about. My students see how hard I work, the genuine interest I show for them and that my concern for their education and their well-being is sincere. I make sure that they feel they are worthy of my time. And, of course, I give them the same respect I expect from them. They will never hear me being sarcastic with them, and I will never, ever belittle them or their efforts. I take care never to underestimate them, and I show them my personal side so that they know my values, my beliefs, who I really am. They know I am human, and I'm not afraid to show them my fear, my anger, or my sadness.

In turn, her students give one hundred percent of themselves. Not only are they not afraid to try new skills, but they are proud to share with her the skills they have mastered. Most of her students would journey to the ends of the earth for her, such is their devotion for a teacher who respects them for who they are, not just for what they can do. She says her philosophy is simple. Achievement does not bring self-esteem—rather build self-esteem and that will bring achievement.

That same philosophy works in her coaching, as well. But, she cautions, the place to start is with the sport itself.

A coach must be skilled, because a coach who is out of his depth will resort to anger and derision instead of critical analysis and decision. A good coach is going to know his players better than they know themselves. And they will trust him. They'll know that coach might put them into a difficult situation, but never an impossible situation. Like when Mario Tremblay left Patrick Roy in net after he had let in something like nine goals. That should never have happened. Tremblay should have pulled Roy, and saved him the humiliation. I will never mould my students, or my players, through fear or guilt or intimidation.

Through example, a good teacher, coach, or parent can make children understand that respect is a very special consideration, a special esteem in which one person holds another. Respect means many things: rising above controversy, standing firm with your convictions, removing yourself from a comfort zone in support of what is right, and ensuring that children are learning what is right, in spite of what others do. These elements form the kind of respect that moves mountains.

FOR PARENTS AND COACHES: RESPECT

Are the children respected as essential and important individuals in your organization? Is respect from the children for adults demanded and commanded rather than earned?

XX: FIFTEENTH PRECEPT

RELIABILITY

"To be relied upon is a greater compliment than to be loved."
— *Anonymous*

Have you ever made plans with someone who cancelled out
at the last minute or simply didn't show up? What about you?
Have you ever changed or cancelled a commitment because
it wasn't convenient for you? When you tell friends that you'll
pick them up at a certain time, or that you'll meet them at
an appointed hour, are you there? Do you keep your prom-
ises?

It's so easy to believe that the others will understand your
reasons for being unable to meet that commitment. You may
even have convinced yourself that your decision is justified.
It's an erroneous assumption. What you really need to be

asking yourself is whether or not you are the kind of person others can count on. Be sure you are honest with yourself when you answer.

Reliable people are conscientious and trustworthy, honouring their commitments whenever humanly possible. They aren't likely to change plans because something better came along. In short, a reliable person can be relied upon by family, co-workers, friends, and even strangers.

Reliability is a quality that children learn through example. If the coach is late, or doesn't show up, anticipation and excitement turn to confusion and bewilderment. Why didn't the coach show up? Yet, if children are surrounded by adults who always honour their commitments, they will grow up understanding the need to keep their word. It's another one of those lessons that can be learned through coaching on the sports field, yet carries into all other aspects of their lives. Only through action can you demonstrate that you are reliable.

If you've made the decision to become a coach, be certain that you can make the time, because commitment requires time. You must be there ahead of the appointed hour for all games and all practices, and make the parents aware that part of their responsibility means that they, too, need to be reliable. Through this mutual example, the children can't help but get the right message. Make it clear to each member of your team that it is his responsibility to let the coach know if he is going to be late or unable to attend. All the talent in the world isn't worth dust if you are not reliable.

FOR PARENTS AND COACHES: RELIABILITY

Are the children encouraged by example to be reliable?
Do coaches and parents act in consistently reliable ways?

XXI: SIXTEENTH PRECEPT—

HOW TO LOSE

"There are some defeats more triumphant than victories."
— *Montaigne*

Do you know how to lose? This is a question every little league coach should ask of him- or herself. I queried a number of coaches and was taken aback by some of the scorn tossed at me. I fielded replies such as:

"Losing is not an option."
"Don't say that word in front of the kids!"
"If we lost, it's because we didn't try hard enough."
"How to lose? Sure, you lose because you play lousy."
"Your not supposed to know how to lose because you don't ever want to get used to losing."

"You don't have to know how to lose, it just happens and you feel lousy about it."

These erroneous, albeit well-meant, comments give us insight into an attitude that is being passed on to thousands of children every day. Although an adult may know how to put such acrimony into perspective, a child certainly does not. A child learns to equate losing with not being good enough.

I have to say, once again, that winning isn't inevitable—losing is! If we never learn how to lose with dignity, life will

Channel that competitive energy positively.

hold many bitter memories for us indeed. Children look to adults for direction and leadership. They believe their coaches know more about the game than their parents do, and if the coach says that losing is for losers, what is a child to think? He will naturally think that he is worthless because the team lost.

There is nothing wrong with losing, so long as we take a lesson from each loss. What we learn may not necessarily make us winners the next time, but it will teach us more about ourselves, and it will move us in a positive direction. Therefore, learning how to lose is just as important as learning how to win, yet so little is understood about the philosophy of losing. It should not be something that you simply tolerate between wins. Losing is not about being less worthy. Children need to believe that losing is a learning experience. We can teach children that losing is a gauge of sorts, a measure for improvement. We should encourage them to try their best and to learn from mistakes. There is nothing wrong with losing as long as you are doing your best.

It's true that as children grow older, winning becomes more important to them. The competitive spirit stirs and grows. It is the job of both parents and coaches to channel that competitive energy positively.

When children involved in any sport or game are having fun while learning, there is no such thing as losing!

FOR PARENTS AND COACHES: LOSING

Are the children being taught to take defeat in stride, to learn from their mistakes, to forget the negativity, and to go on to the next aspect of struggle? Are they learning that perseverance always wins? Are they rewarded for actual effort and attempts, rather than punished for "losing"?

XXII: SEVENTEENTH PRECEPT—
RESPONSIBILITY

"The things which must be, must be for the best,
...to do our duty... humbly..." — Owen Meredith

For the most part, the ideas contained in this book are based on my own observations and experiences with little league players and coaches, and I have used these for my arguments. Responsibility, however, is such an important part of life that it requires more in-depth reflection. Accepting responsibility is a vital part of any child's development and will determine the usefulness of their role within society.

Who *is* responsible for what a child learns? One might answer teachers, of course. But if we think about the different areas of learning, we must certainly look beyond teachers, for their influence on children is confined to a finite period of time. Yes, they teach the basics of reading, writing and arithmetic, and more specific skills and concepts as children progress to higher levels, and they work to instil a general code of ethics and moral behaviour. But a teacher is just one of many who will walk through a child's life.

A child's well-being is the responsibility of parents or guardians, foremost. In supporting roles is an entire cast of individuals— relatives, friends, religious leaders, family doctors, and, of course, coaches. In fact, anyone who spends any amount of time with that child, anyone the child views in a position of authority, bears responsibility to that child— though admittedly the ultimate weight falls on the shoulders of the parents. Where your child is concerned, "the buck stops here."

We are living in an age of blame. We want someone to blame for all the ills of the world— crime, unemployment, poverty, environmental pollution, and social unrest and conflict. We blame television, the movies, newspapers, magazines, rock groups and government. We even blame each other.

After four consecutive days of rain, I overheard someone say: "That stupid weather girl said the sun would shine today, and it's raining again!" Is the weather announcer to blame for the rain?

It comes, then, as no surprise that responsibility ranked but seventeenth on our list of lessons that children should learn through minor sports.

As I listen to the news, or read a magazine or newspaper, it seems that fewer and fewer people are willing to accept responsibility for their own actions. The headline read *Fog Responsible for Ten-car Pile-up*. This conjures an image of a giant hand made out of fog reaching out and pushing cars into one another. A responsible person adjusts to inclement weather conditions, or simply stays at home. It's about choice and ensuing consequences. Whether or not you chose to drive in the fog is a decision that rests entirely with you, and, although there may be outside forces influencing your decision, you must bear the responsibility of your choice.

We all make hundreds of decisions every day, the consequences of which depend on circumstances. Our actions are based on our own experiences and motivations, and it's important that children learn that each decision bears a consequence.

Recently, the media reported on the tragic story of a seven-year-old girl who attempted to fly across the United States and back, accompanied by her father and her flight instructor. We heard, read or listened to the telling and retelling of a gifted child who had learned to fly a light aircraft. She was attempting to set a flying record, which, were she successful, would have brought her fame and financial reward, likely through product endorsement. We accept the story at face value that while attempting to take off in inclement weather, they crashed. She tried, she failed, she died. Many of us cried for that precocious little girl, and viewed her premature death as one of life's tragedies.

But there is much this story misses. Some questioned risking the life of a child for a record, and others wondered why children are allowed to fly airplanes. Psychologist Allan

Goebel wrote an analysis of the incident with regard to responsibility, which appeared in the local newspaper. In it he asked some uncomfortable questions and drew some nasty conclusions, echoing the feelings of many of us who followed the story.

Jessica Dubroff, seven, is dead, along with her father and flight instructor. Jessica's mother is quoted as saying that she would want all her children to 'die in a state of joy.' I suspect that although Jessica loved flying and wanted to fly until she died, she likely died in a state of fear and confusion. She may have died wondering what had gone wrong, and wondering why the adults with her weren't protecting her or making things better.

In what I read about Jessica's death, I don't recall any emphasis on responsibility, protecting children from harm and taking only calculated risks.

What was so important to them that required them to have Jessica take off in conditions that would have tested the skill of an adult, veteran pilot?

Was her flying instructor trying to promote himself while allowing Jessica to take off under dangerous conditions? Was her father trying to validate his beliefs about child-rearing or was he trying to bask in reflected glory while encouraging a seven-year-old child to set a meaningless record? Didn't Jessica's mother realize she was putting Jessica and others at risk by allowing Jessica to explore, experiment, be free and just live her life?

As a society we need laws that prevent parents and organizations from exploiting children by putting them into dangerous, record-setting situations.

As parents we need to monitor ourselves constantly to ensure we don't sacrifice our children to promote our own values and ideas.

We need to remember that training is progressive, long-term and systematic. We need to be patient enough to do this training.

It is not only possible but imperative to draw a parallel between this alleged exploitation of a child to that of the obsession to win in little league. One might argue that it is ludicrous to equate the death of a small child with that of the potential hurt and humiliation a child might endure from a determined coach or overzealous parents. I heartily disagree and further assert that the damage some children experience through little league is life-long and debilitating. Our letters have proven this.

A newborn child is utterly dependent on his or her parents. As children learn to walk and talk they begin the long journey to independence. Along the way they learn to judge for themselves and make their own decisions until, one day, the bird leaves the nest. But in the interim a child needs to be governed, and the task is not an easy one. Every parent knows how easy it is to allow a child to do as he wishes— to say "no!" incites confrontation and argument with the corollary being unwanted stress. Yet, there are times we simply must say no. Carol Burnett once said, "You've got to love your kids enough to let them hate you for a while."

Today's children are tomorrow's adults, yet there is increasing concern that we have lost control over a generation of young people. Are the children to blame or are they merely a product of their environment? An environment that we, the adults, have created? Do we accept responsibility for their errant attitudes?

Make mistakes a learning experience.

Who is responsible for what a child learns? Whatever your role is— teacher, parent, coach— the truth is that we are all responsible for what children learn.

FOR PARENTS AND COACHES: RESPONSIBILITY

Are coaches and parents taking true responsibility for their own actions? Do they understand the relationship between the examples that they provide and the behaviour of their charges? Is true responsibility on the part of the children rewarded?

XXIII: EIGHTEENTH PRECEPT—
SETTING GOALS

"Our deeds determine us, as much as we determine our deeds." — George Eliot

Have you ever thought about what your goals in life are? How many people struggle through the week just to make it to the weekend, or struggle through the year for two weeks of holiday. Lived like that, life can be tedious.

My life was shaken to its roots when I had the good fortune of attending a weekend self-improvement seminar some years ago. It brought me to the rude awakening that I was one of those people who struggled through the week to make it to the weekend. What I learned about setting goals changed my life.

Having goals gives us something to strive for. It creates ambition and affords us a sense of direction. Getting up each day is so much more meaningful when you have plans and ideas to look forward to. This concept can be applied to children, as well, but because children do not understand life's complexities as adults do, you need to help children in setting individual goals. Explore the capabilities of each child and then help him set realistic goals. This is not as difficult as it sounds.

Sean, from Massachusetts, writes of a good memory from his childhood.

I was in the forth or fifth grade and playing some form of dodge ball at recess. We had mothers as recess monitors. It was general practice for those of us not as athletically inclined as others to surrender the ball to the 'best' player on the team if we happened to get hold of it. This practice benefited the team because the best player had a much better chance of getting an 'out.' The obvious problem is that it reduced children like myself to the status of water boy.

One particular day I got the ball and looked for the 'best' player to pass it to. As I stood, searching, the recess monitor asked me what I was doing. I told her I was looking for the 'best player.' 'THROW THE BALL YOUR-SELF' was her instant and loud reply.

*I have no idea what happened then. I do know I threw the ball, and I do know I never again gave it to the 'best player.' I am totally without recollection of the outcome of the play. I only know that I threw it **myself**!*

I played two sports in high school, captained my soccer team in college and went on to be an NCAA Division II head coach. *I have been in leadership positions all my life and I have always remembered that moment. How would my life have turned out had she not yelled at me to throw the ball? I say a resounding 'Thank you, recess mother,' and wish that I could thank her today. If all of us could have the same clear vision... 'just play the game and do*

...a moment that Sean will remember forever.

your best'... what a wonderful time the children of all ages would have. What a great generation of leaders we could raise.

A moment of chance and Sean's life was changed forever. He set higher goals for himself. A stranger gave Sean a choice he never realized he had, and it became the turning point of his life.

Will your coaching style be the turning point in some child's life that builds self-esteem, confidence and character, or will you be the reason he never reaches full potential?

It is uncanny how children remember moments from their past as though these were locked in time. As a coach you have the power to build a child up or knock him down. My own experiences and observations have demonstrated to me just how true this is. Recently, I accompanied a friend to his son Josh's soccer game. If you enjoy watching children at play, watch five-year-olds play soccer. Although this was the last game of the season, the emphasis was not on winning. Josh and his teammates played hard, had riotous fun and as a reward for their efforts, were treated to pizza. To Josh, this was the highlight of the season. There were unabashed smiles and giggles from all the children. Winning the World Cup would not have made them any happier. That day Josh set a goal for himself. The following year he would play soccer again, and at the end of the season he would share pizza with him teammates.

Of course, as Josh gets older, his goals will change. Young children have such simple goals, and that's as it should be.

Proper perspective is necessary when setting goals for children. Had Josh's coach set a goal of winning the championship instead of having fun and learning the game, Josh might have had a very different kind of memory.

It is imperative to remember that goals need to be attainable and then recognized when achieved. Even if it's just pizza for five-year-old soccer players.

FOR PARENTS AND COACHES: SETTING GOALS

At the beginning of the season have each player set an objective for himself and write it down. It may simply be to catch one fly ball or to get a single assist. Or, for someone who is especially skilled, an appropriate goal might be to become MVP for the season.

It is probable that some children will suggest winning as their goal. You need to make them understand that winning is perhaps a team goal, but not an individual goal, and as a team goal it is an indirect objective rather than their main purpose.

Goals need to be practicable. When a child succeeds in reaching his goal, applaud that success. Make a big deal of it. That child needs to feel a sense of accomplishment for having the necessary motivation and perseverance. As a coach, when you acknowledge the achievement, you are contributing to the development of that child in a most positive manner by creating a memory that will stay with him for years to come. With one success comes another, and another, and yet another, so that many years from now he will still be setting realistic goals for himself.

XXIV: NINETEENTH PRECEPT—

RESILIENCE

"We shall escape the uphill by never turning back."
— *Christina G. Rossetti*

We have all seen incidents which cause people to react in different ways. Some people get angry over the weather, while others simply take it in stride. Some wait patiently at a red light, and others fume.

Have you ever wondered why some people become annoyed easily and others seem to possess the patience of Job? The child failed to score on a breakaway or perhaps struck out with the tying run on third base. There are some parents who react with anger and shout at the child. But there are parents who react only with encouragement. What do you do?

People who remain calm in uncomfortable situations are

confident that things will improve. They believe that misfortune, whether it be a rainy day, a red light, a missed goal, a strike-out or even a job setback, is only temporary. They will bounce back. They are resilient.

Children react differently, too, to given situations. Very young children usually just shrug off a mistake and carry on. They may not even realize that they have made a mistake until the coach tells them or someone yells at them. As children get older, they recognise personal mistakes and when they do, they are hardest on themselves. In sports they feel dreadful about letting the team down. And a win-at-all-costs coach will make them feel even worse. All of a sudden the game becomes serious and the fun is gone.

Imagine you are a ten-year-old child excited about being in the game. Your parents are there watching for the very first time. It's your big moment to make the play, but, oh no, you make a mistake! You feel terrible about it. You want to cry, then Dad yells, "It's okay! Get back in the game, John!"

That's encouragement.

Coaches and parents alike need to be aware that what children need most when they make a mistake is support and encouragement. We have all heard the cliché, "If, at first, you don't succeed, try, try again." The message is one of resilience. A child who makes a mistake needs to learn from it, forget the negativity, and get on with the task at hand. Positive encouragement from the coach goes a long way to building confidence in children. Coaches must promote the idea that mistakes are learning experiences. Children who believe this won't be afraid to try new challenges. They will set higher goals for themselves. As children grow older and make mistakes— and they will make mistakes— chances are that they will shrug them off, just as they did when they were three years old. It's up to you to help create the resilience which will lead to self-confidence.

Major league pitcher Jim Abbott, who has only one hand, is an excellent example of resilience. It would have been so easy for him to give up and play the victim his whole life. Instead he chose to persevere, and pursue his dream in spite of his so-called handicap. This is one man who likely received a hearty helping of support and encouragement in his formative years. He is a modern-day hero and a lesson to us all.

Terry Fox, who ran across Canada with only one leg, raising money for cancer research, is an example of supreme heroism. Rick Hansen, the Olympic cyclist who was paralyzed in an accident and who has dedicated his life to educating others about disabilities, has risen above events and transcended his accident. Canadian Olympic gold-medal rower Silken Laumann, severely injured in a boating accident in which her calf muscle was nearly cut in half, persevered to come back in only a few months and compete in the Olympics.

An ultimate example of resilience is the actor, Christopher Reeve— Superman to millions of fans. When an equestrian accident left him with a broken neck, unable to move any part of his body, not able to breathe for himself, he did not want to go on living. Through the love, support and encouragement of his family, he came back more determined than ever. His struggle is not an easy one, each day being a trial of survival, yet he has signed contracts to direct since the accident happened. He is committed to going on with his life and his work, and to doing everything in his power to raise awareness and the necessary funding for spinal injury research. One must look at Mr. Reeve and say, "If this man can be so resilient after such a devastating injury, it is within every person's power to be so."

FOR PARENTS AND COACHES: RESILIENCE

Are children being taught resilience— the inner strength to bounce back— or are they being "toughened" in a way that makes them rigid and impossibly perfectionist?

XXV: TWENTIETH PRECEPT—
PERSPECTIVE

"For some must follow, and some must command
Though all are made of clay!" — *Longfellow*

"From the error of others, a wise man corrects his own."
— *Syrus*

While this may be the shortest of the precepts contained in this book, it is probably the most important of all. Throughout this guide, you have probably caught glimpses of yourself in the words. If nothing else, I hope I have shown that your influence on the children you coach is direct and commanding. That means the responsibility you have undertaken is really quite awesome. Remember that children who sign up to play little league sports just want to have fun, especially when they are young, and that is what your focus must be.

You must put that into an overall perspective of character development for each young life that you touch. Chances are, when dealing with children, if there is a problem, your focus is on winning and you have lost true perspective.

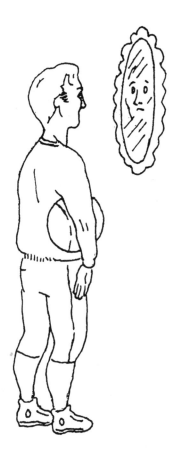

Don't judge him too harshly lest you recognize him in the mirror...

If there is even a little of Coach Eddie in the way you do things, it is time to reconsider. You need to put things in proper perspective. After all, even Coach Eddie was able to change, and if he can, so can you. How do I know that Coach Eddie has changed?

Coach Eddie wrote this book.

FOR PARENTS AND COACHES: PERSPECTIVE

Are teams managed and led as if they were adult professional teams? Do coaches expect obedient little machines in their players, or are their relationships human and encouraging? Are the children happy when they practice, happy when they play, and happy after games, regardless of whether or not they won?

XXVI: CONCLUSION

"Children have more need of models than of critics."
— Joubert

It seems very long ago that I first asked that all-important question that led to this book. I asked: "What should coaches be teaching children?" A simple question that produced hundreds of not-so-simple replies.

It has been said that to be the best you can be you must combine skill with a positive attitude. When I asked seminar participants, coaches, and parents to define whether each precept referred to a skill or an attitude, the overwhelming response favoured attitude. This holds true in sports as well as in life. The message is very clear. Eighty-five percent of what you teach children should be about the right attitude.

A coach's job, albeit voluntary, goes far beyond passing on athletic skills. You must be part psychologist, part philosopher, part confidant, part teacher— the complete role model. Tough gig, isn't it?

Not at all, if you maintain the right attitude. Maybe you thought showing up and winning were enough. Not only are they non-starters, they demonstrate a philosophy that can be detrimental to the development of a child.

There will always be children who possess exceptional skills with major league potential. Exceptional skill will never be the reason for failure to make it to the major leagues, but a bad attitude could very easily lead to failure.

The game is over. We lost. But the little leaguers are smiling and munching pizza. The smiles are your reward. They tell you that the children are happy. Their smiles are proof that there is such a thing as...

...winning without winning!

FOR PARENTS AND COACHES: CONCLUSION

If you have carefully followed your list of what coaches should be teaching throughout this book and made notes about your own organization's good and not-so-good aspects, you will already have a much clearer idea of where work needs to be done. It's a good idea to prioritize this list, and begin the slow process of altering the organization from within, and *by your own example.* Sometimes elements of improvement can be made simply by talking to a fellow coach or to your child's coach. Sometimes what will be needed is a set of organizational objectives that can be provided to all the coaches and parents as models for improvement in various areas.

Keep in mind that blaming and anger are not the answers. Coaches are human, too. Sometimes coaches flounder because of inadequate training or a lack of direction about what parents and minor sports organizations want them to teach. Support, instruction and consultation are very important for coaches as well.

Working on attitude, on one important element at a time, and deeply understanding the responsibilities of coaches and parents in minor sports over time can transform an organization and make it a truly wonderful and fulfilling place for the children involved in it.

ABOUT THE AUTHOR

GERRY CROWLEY, minor sports consultant and coach, has spent many years working with kids, coaches and parents in seminars and in coaching, as well as at the organizational level, to develop positive environments for children. Crowley spent more than four years researching and writing this book. He lives in Kitchener, Ontario, with his wife, Catherine, and their children.